21st Century
Basic Skills
Library

I KNOW
BASEBALL

3

by Joanne Mattern

Cherry Lake Publishing • Ann Arbor, Michigan

Published in the United States of America
by Cherry Lake Publishing
Ann Arbor, Michigan
www.cherrylakepublishing.com

Consultant: Marla Conn, Read-Ability

Photo Credits: iStockphoto/Thinkstock, cover, 1, 10; Ffooter/Shutterstock,
4; Richard Paul Kane/Shutterstock, 6, 12; Bull's-Eye Arts/Shutterstock,
8; Comstock/Thinkstock, 14; AP Images, 16; Library of Congress, 18; Ted
Mathias/AP Images, 20

Library of Congress Cataloging-in-Publication Data
Mattern, Joanne, 1963-
  I know baseball / Joanne Mattern.
    pages cm. -- (I know sports)
  ISBN 978-1-62431-397-4 (hardcover) -- ISBN 978-1-62431-473-5 (pbk.) --
ISBN 978-1-62431-435-3 (pdf) -- ISBN 978-1-62431-511-4 (ebook)
  1. Baseball--Juvenile literature. I. Title.
  GV867.5.M386 2013
  796.357--dc23
                                        2013006121

Cherry Lake Publishing would like to acknowledge
the work of The Partnership for 21st Century Skills.
Please visit *www.p21.org* for more information.

Printed in the United States of America
Corporate Graphics Inc.
July 2013
CLFA11

TABLE OF CONTENTS

Rules

A baseball game has two teams. Nine players from one team are on the field. Players from the other team bat one at a time.

The batting team tries to score **runs**. One team bats until it gets three **outs**. Then it is the other team's turn.

A baseball game has nine **innings**. The team with the most runs at the end of the game is the winner.

Playing the Game

The pitcher throws the ball to the batter. The pitcher stands on a **mound**. The mound is the highest spot on the field.

The batter stands next to home plate. He swings the bat to try to hit the ball. He tries to get on **base**.

14

There are three bases plus home plate. The batting team tries to get a player around the bases. A run is scored when he gets to home plate.

Records

Barry Bonds hit 762 home runs. Hank Aaron hit 755 home runs. Babe Ruth hit 714 home runs. They are the home run kings.

Cy Young won 511 games as a pitcher. This has been a **record** since 1911.

Cal Ripken Jr. played in 2,632 straight games. He is called "the Iron Man."

Find Out More

BOOK
Burdick, Mason. *Baseball*. New York: Gareth Stevens, 2012.

WEB SITE
Sports Illustrated Kids
www.sikids.com
This Web site has articles about professional baseball and its
   players.

Glossary

base (BASE) one of the places batters must run to in order to
   score

innings (IN-ings) parts of a baseball game during which each
   team bats

mound (MOUND) a small hill a pitcher stands on during a
   baseball game

outs (OUTS) a baseball team gets three and then stops batting

record (REK-urd) a thing that has been done better than
   anyone else

runs (RUHNS) scores in baseball made by touching the three
   bases and reaching home plate

Home and School Connection

Use this list of words from the book to help your child become a better reader. Word games and writing activities can help beginning readers reinforce literacy skills.

baseball	home	pitcher	teams
bat	innings	plate	three
batter	kings	record	throws
batting	man	runs	time
end	most	score	try
field	mound	spot	turn
full	nine	stands	two
game	one	straight	winner
hit	outs	swings	

Index

About the Author

Joanne Mattern has written lots of books about baseball players. She has been a baseball fan since she was a little girl. Her family likes to go to baseball games every summer.